Wat Phra Kaew, or Temple of the Emerald Buddha, is Thailand's primary and most important temple.

Inthakin Festival, Chiang Mai

Wat Phra That Lampang Luang, Lampang

Wat Phumin, Nan

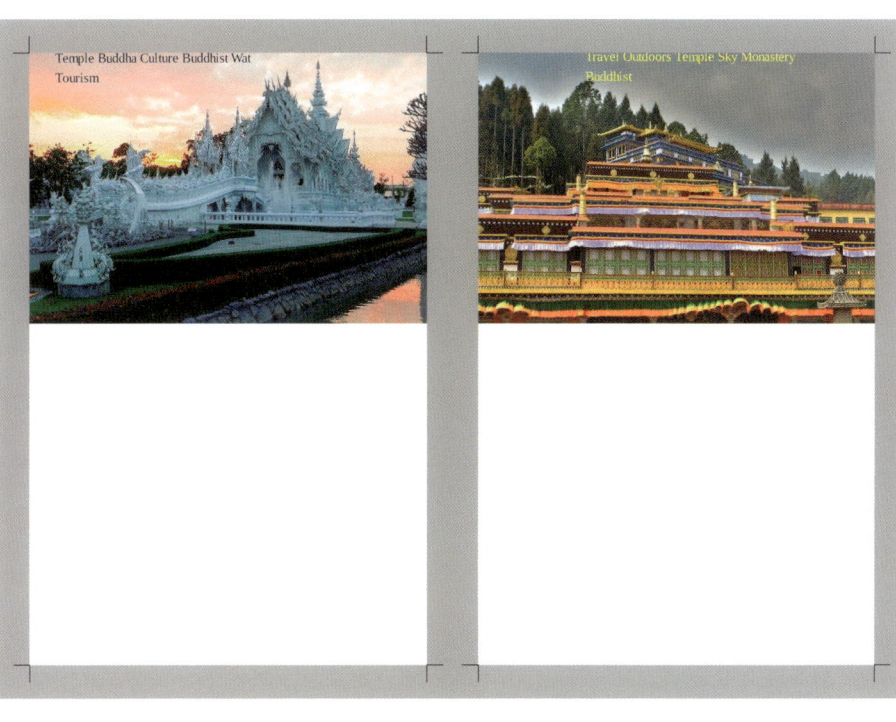

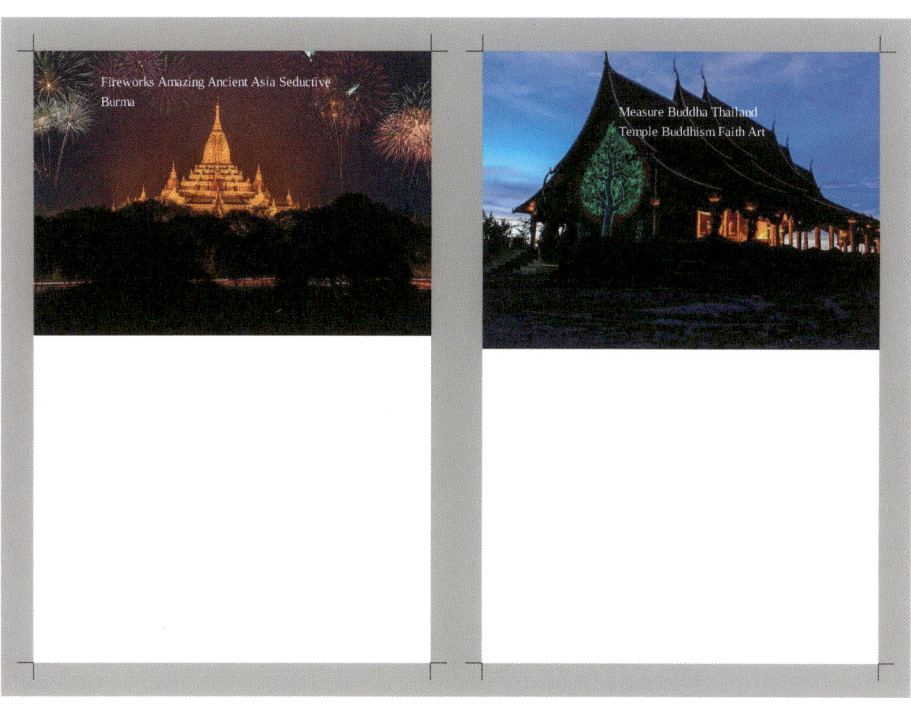

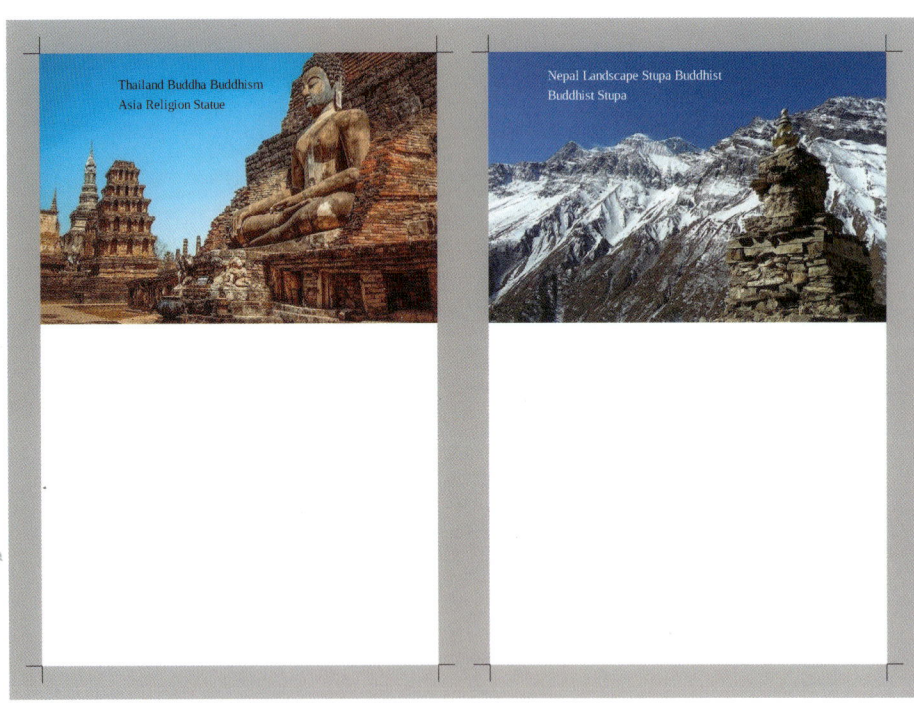

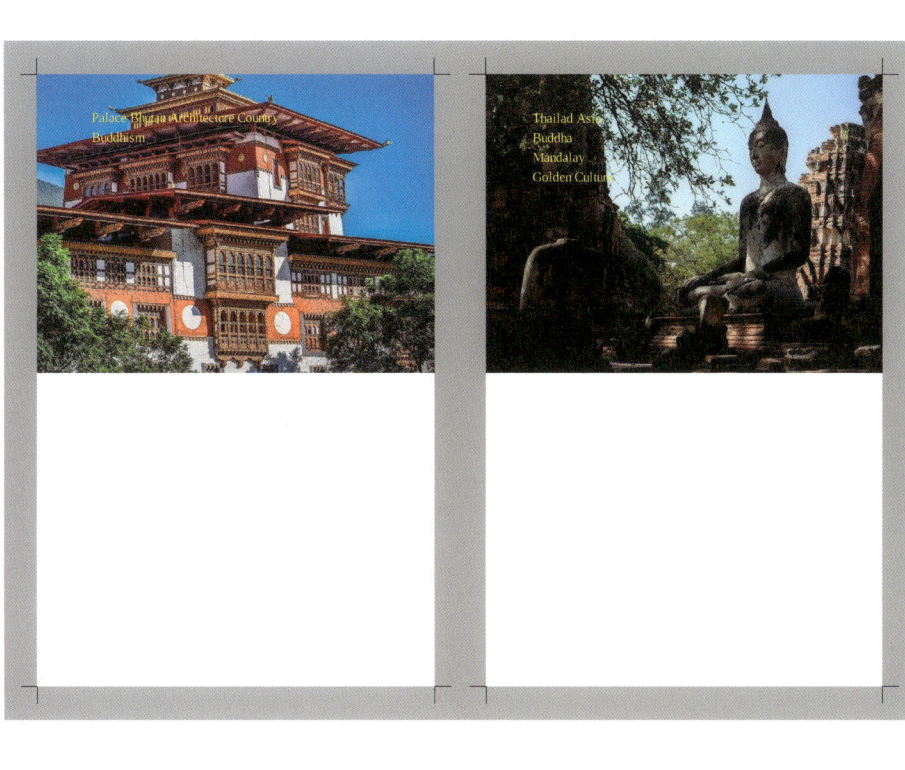

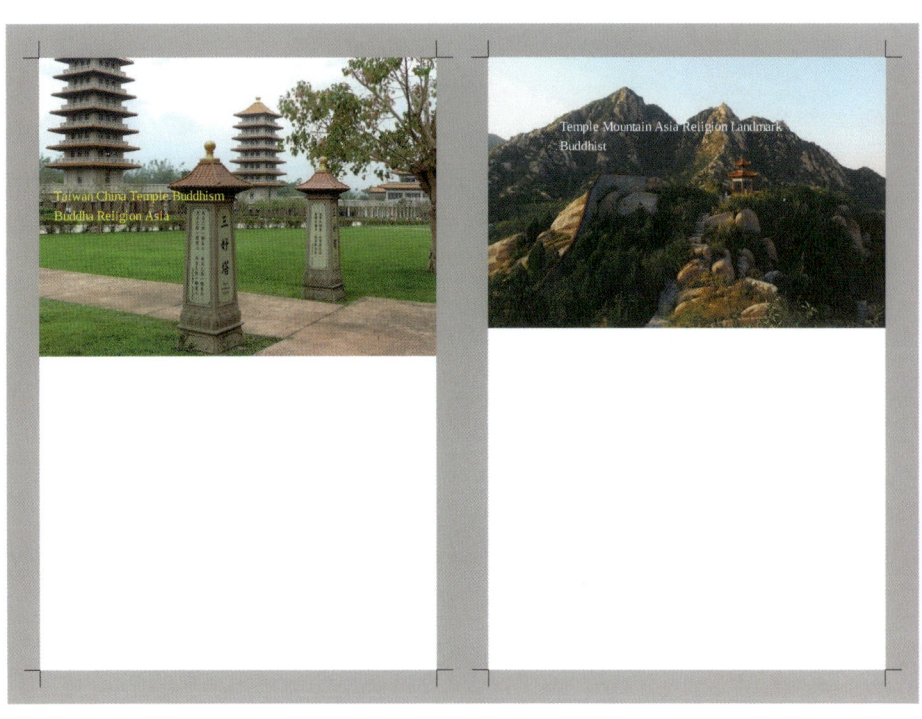

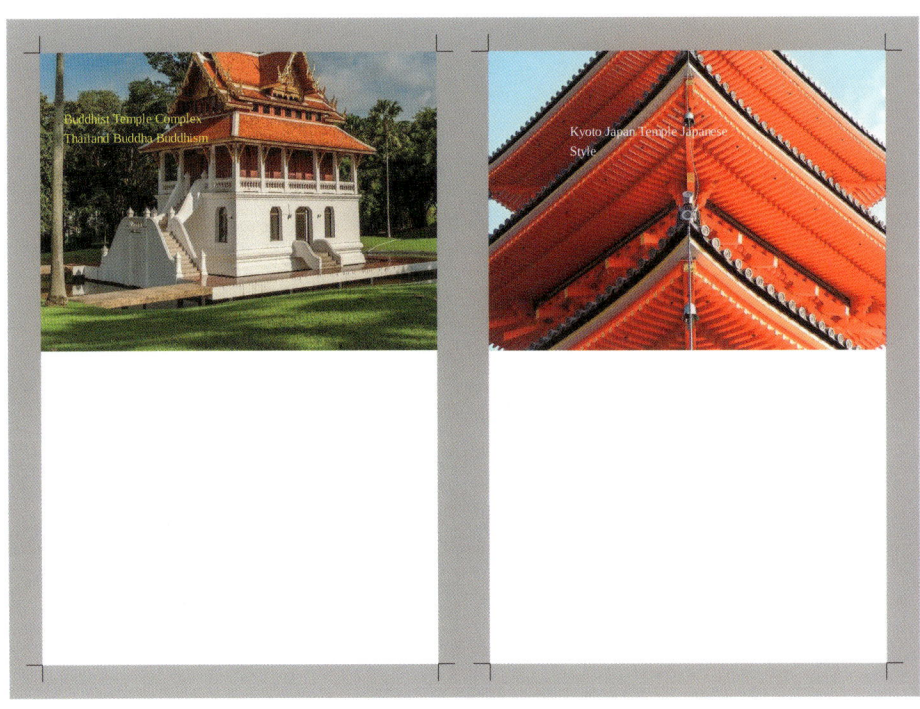

Buddhist Architecture

Wat Xieng Thong Buddhist Temple Temple Monastery

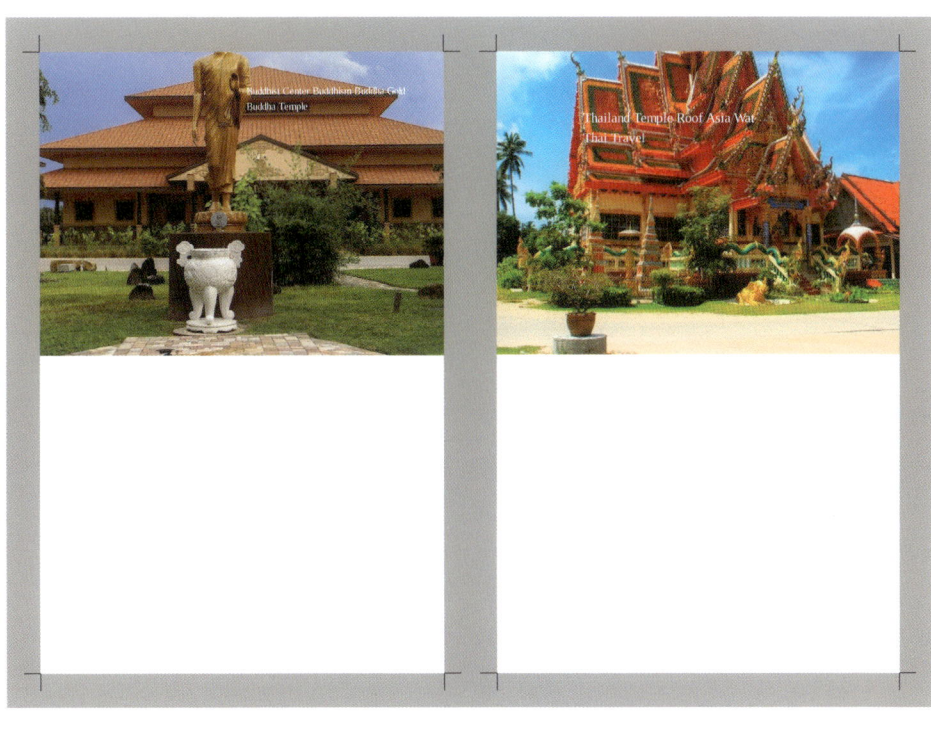

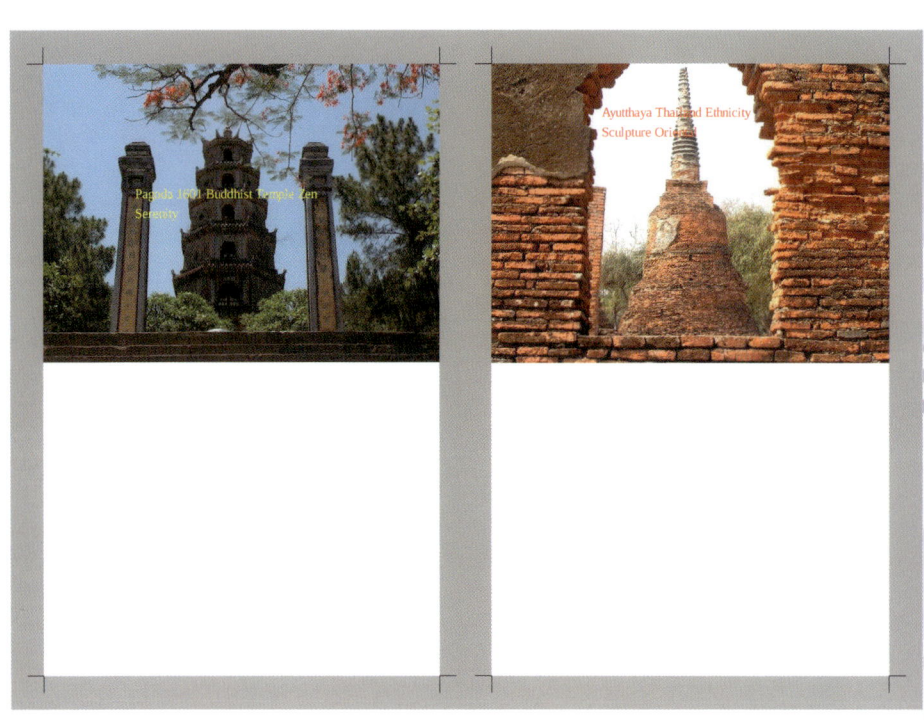

Dochula Pass Monument Stupa Shanti Stupa
Buddhism

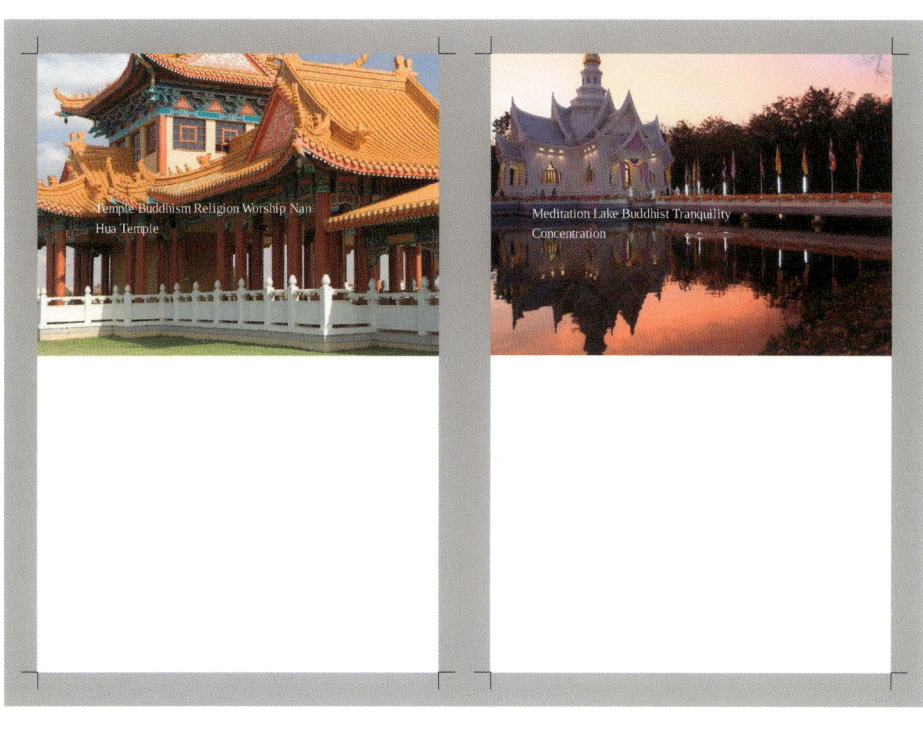

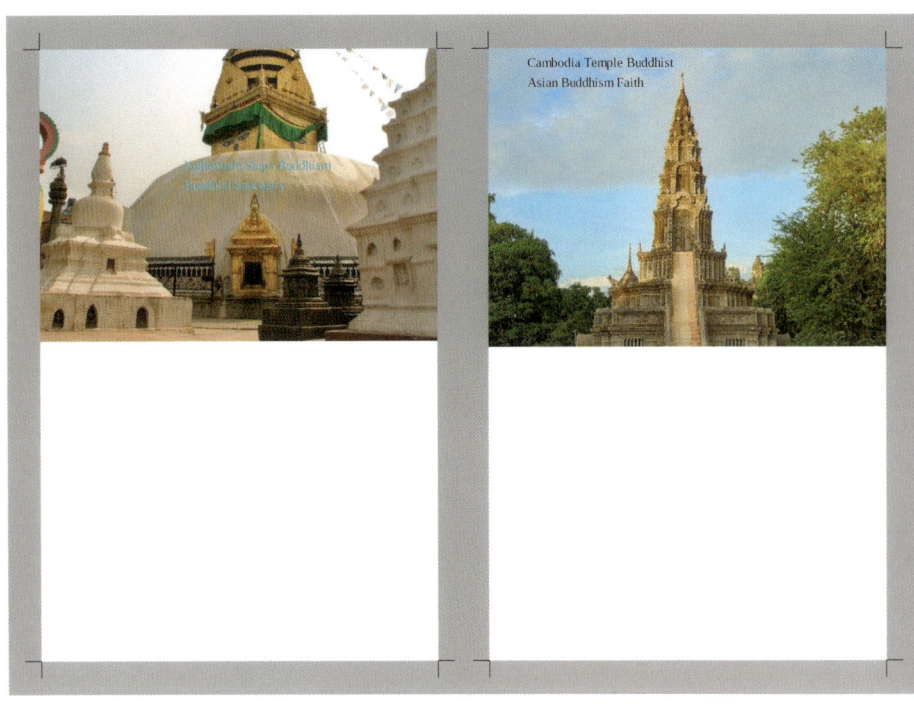

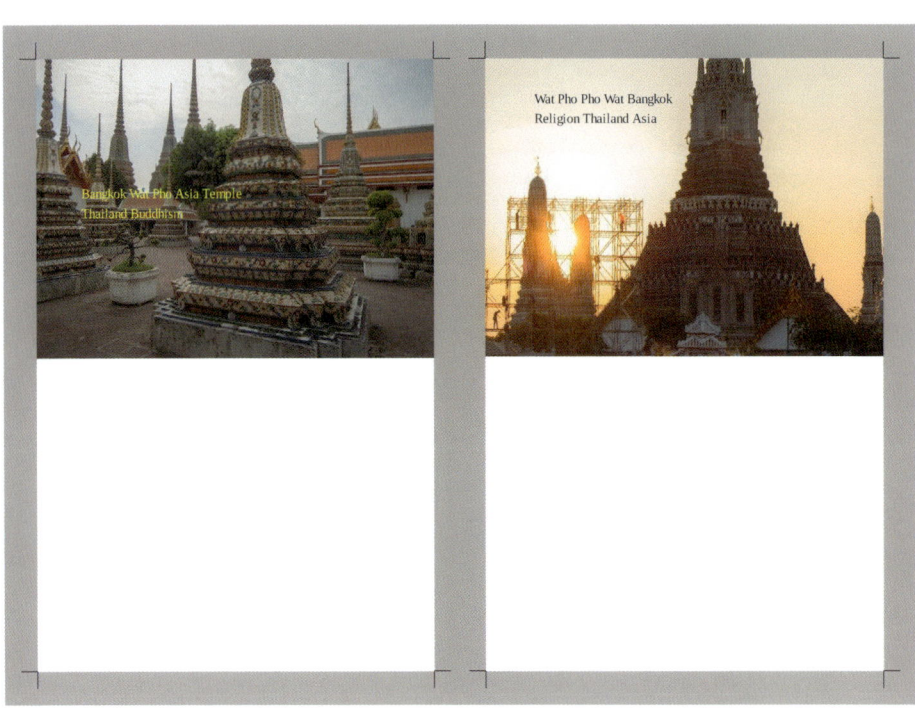

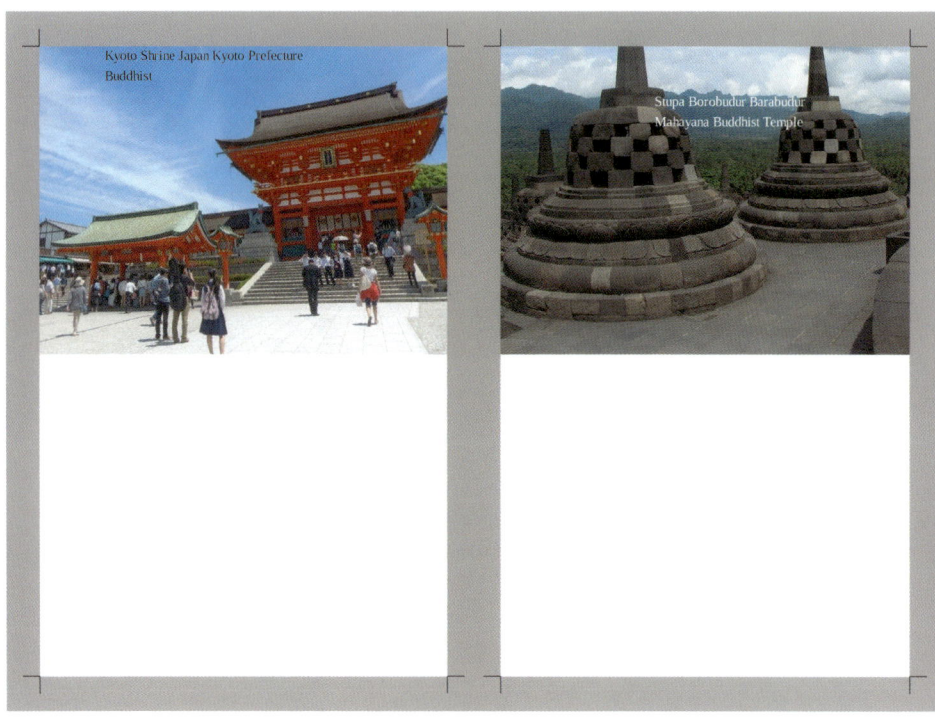

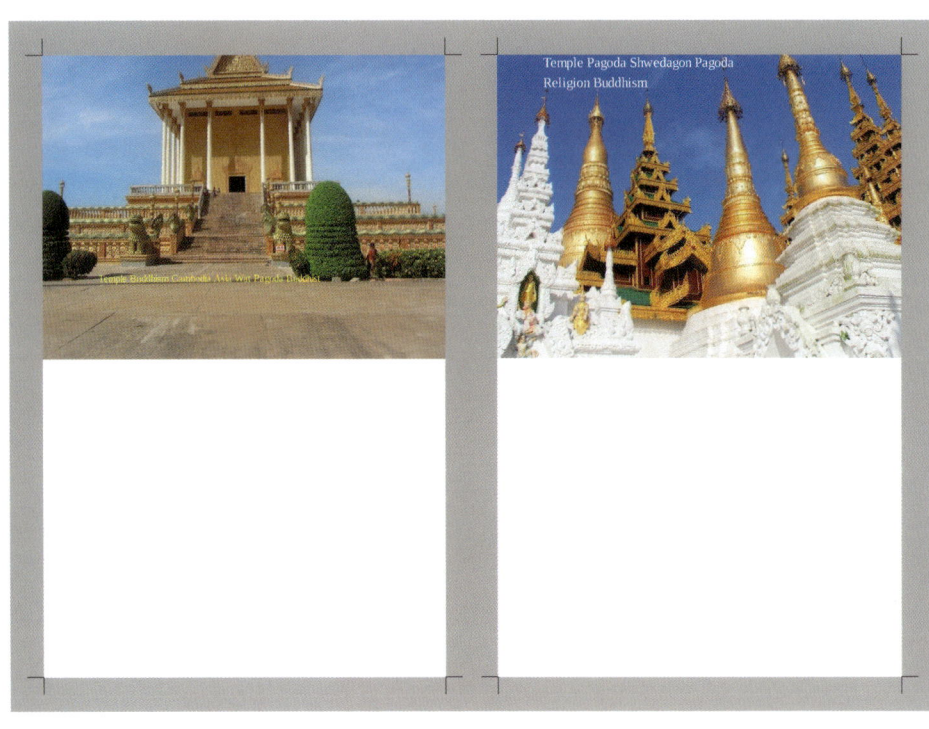

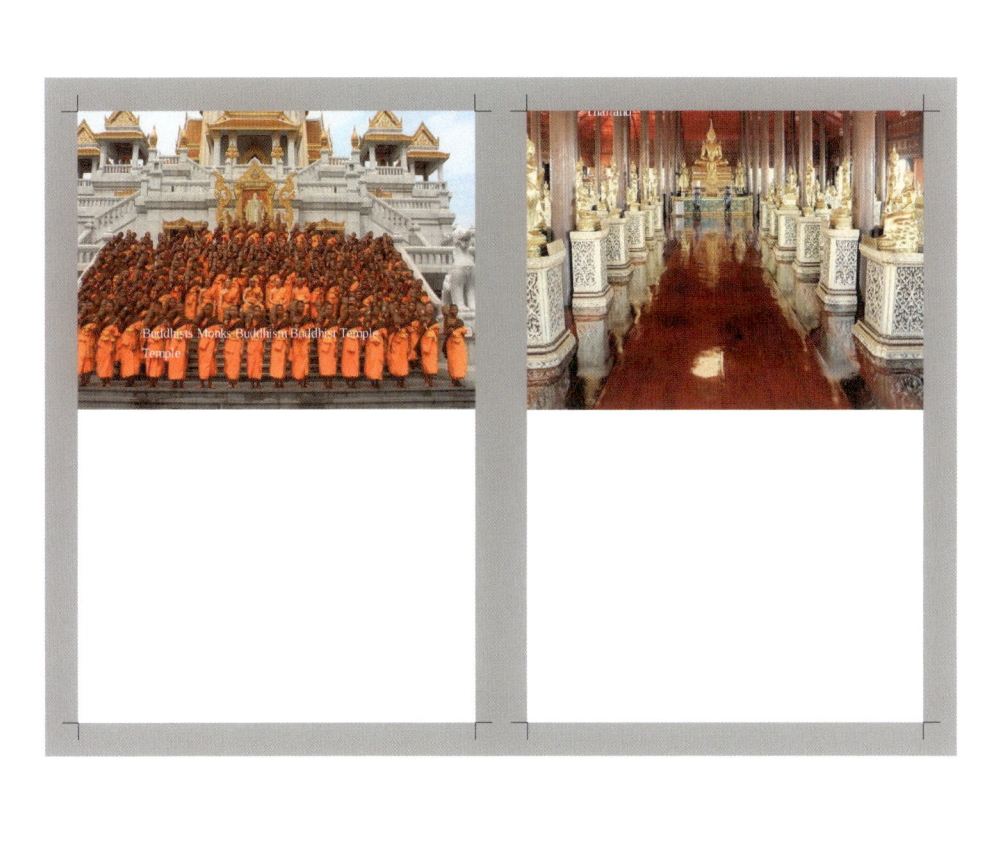

Buddhists Monks Buddhism Buddhist Temple
Temple

Thailand…

Temple Laos Roof Top Asia Buddhism Religion

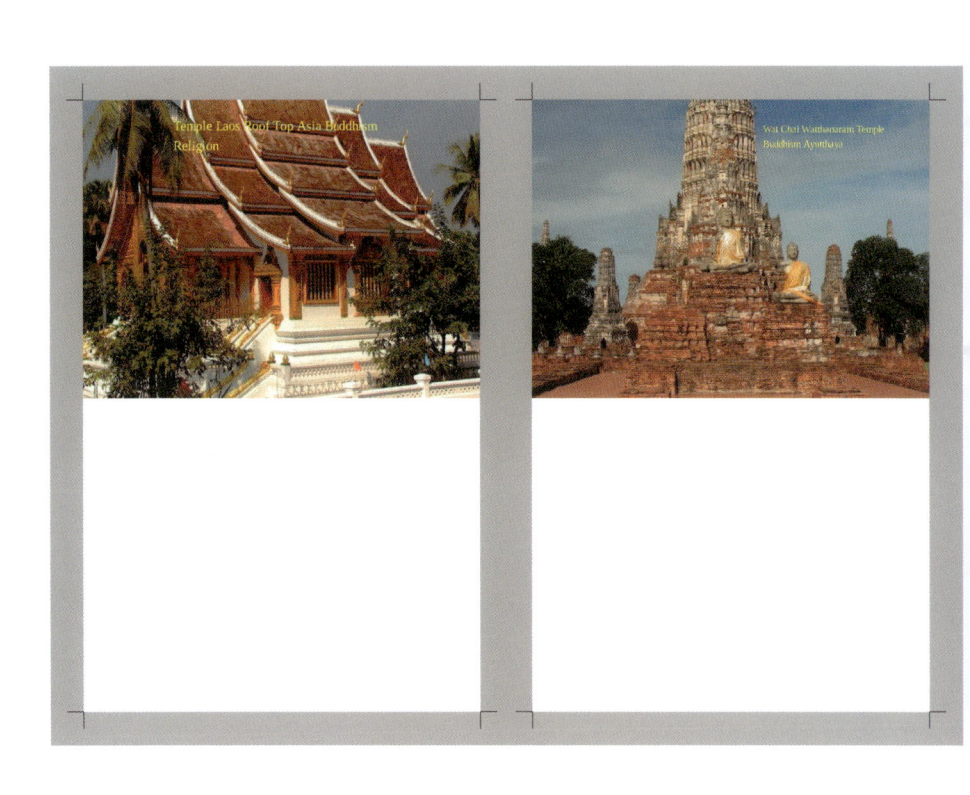

Wat Chai Watthanaram Temple Buddhism Ayutthaya

Concentration

Temple Buddhism Pagoda Buddhist Temple Complex

Thailand Buddhist Temple
Faith Religion Building

Asian Thailand Cambodia
Roof Temple Religion

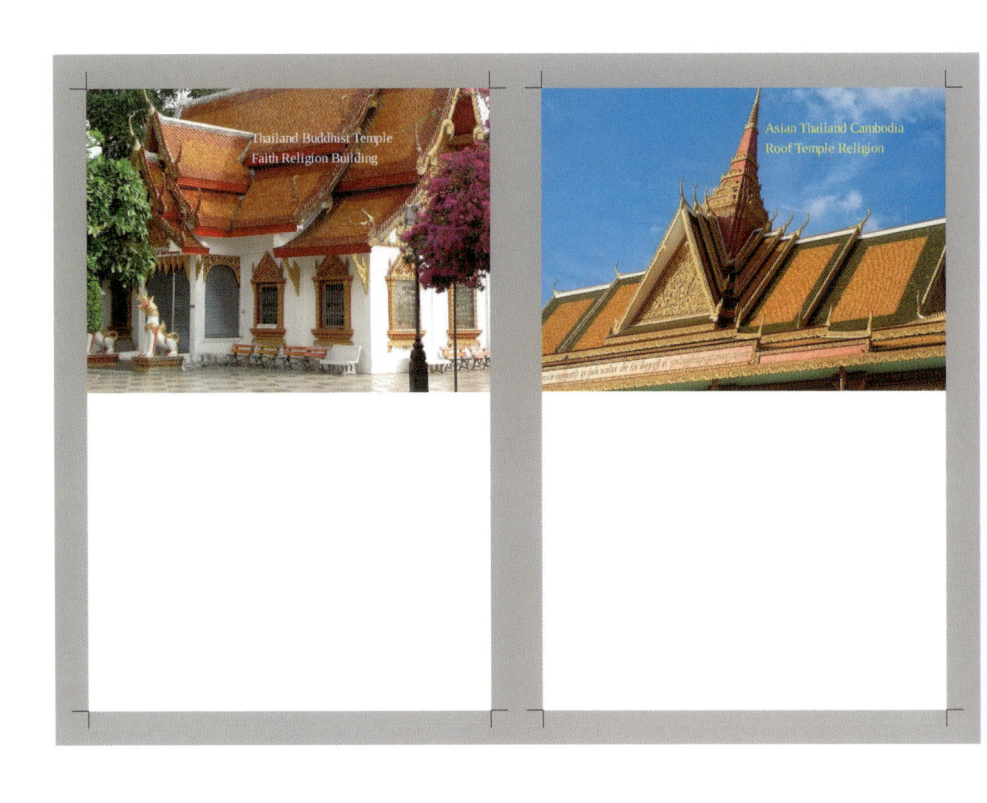

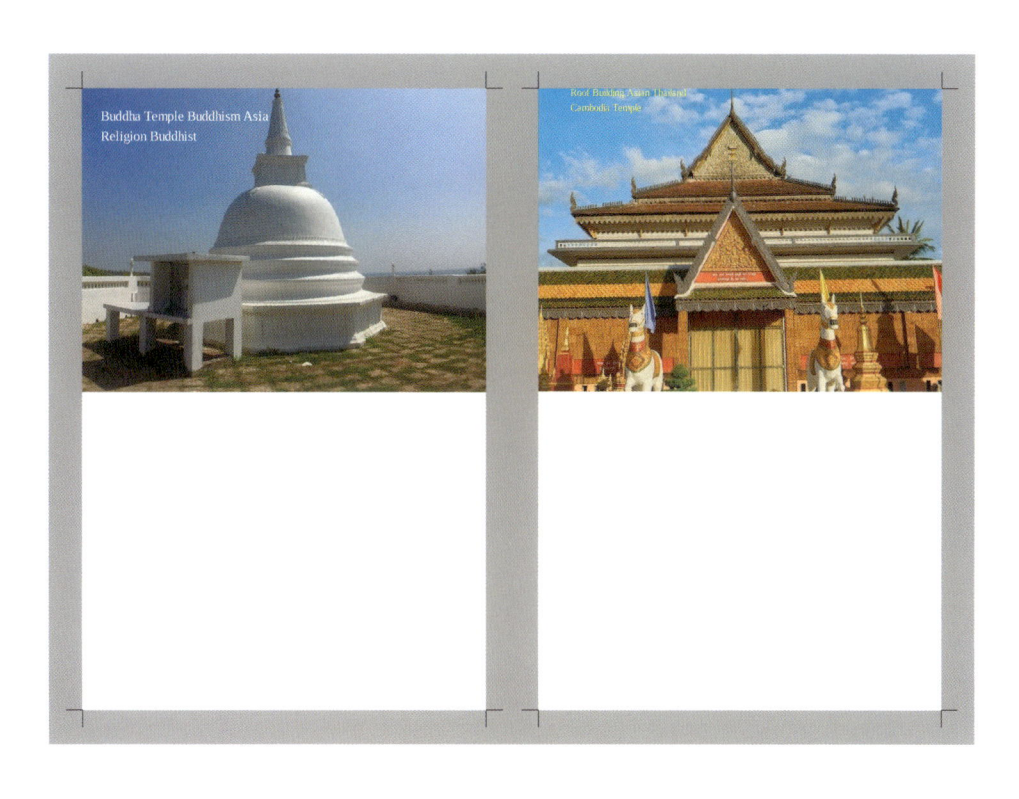

Buddha Temple Buddhism Asia
Religion Buddhist

Roof Building Asian Thailand
Cambodia Temple

Temple Pagoda Buddhist Architecture History Ruins

Old Pagoda Ancient Temple Architecture Asia

Monastery Architecture Ancient Traditional
Landmark

Stupa Candi Brobudur
Magelang Java Indonesia

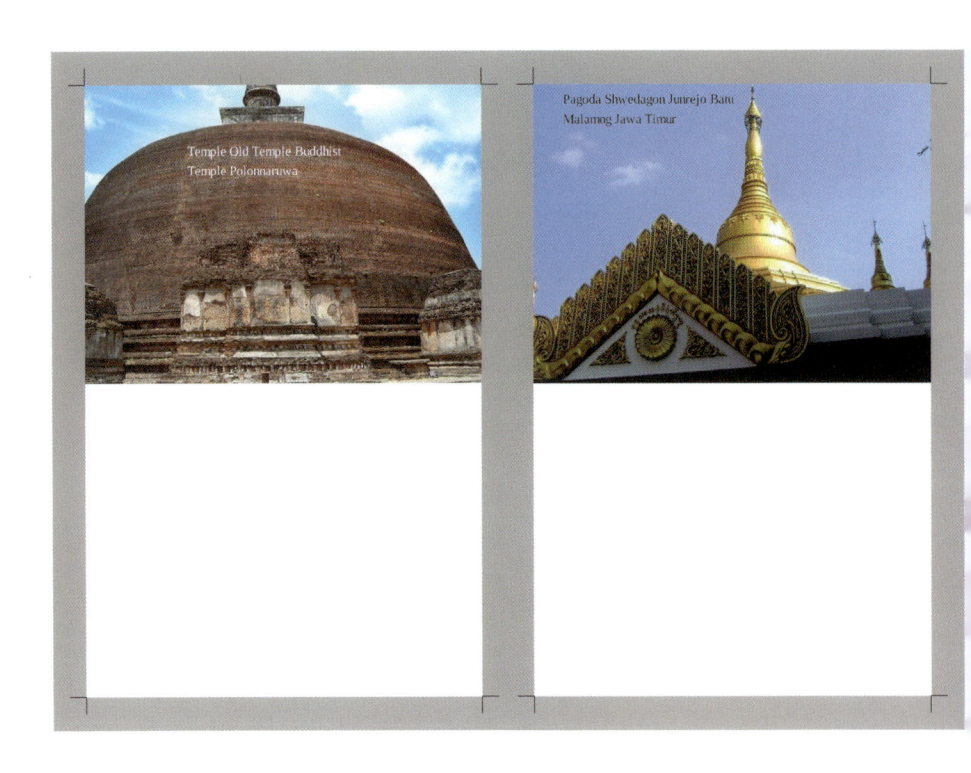

Temple Old Temple Buddhist Temple Polonnaruwa

Pagoda Shwedagon Junrejo Batu Malamog Jawa Timur

Pagoda Thailand Buddhists
Gold Buddhism Thai

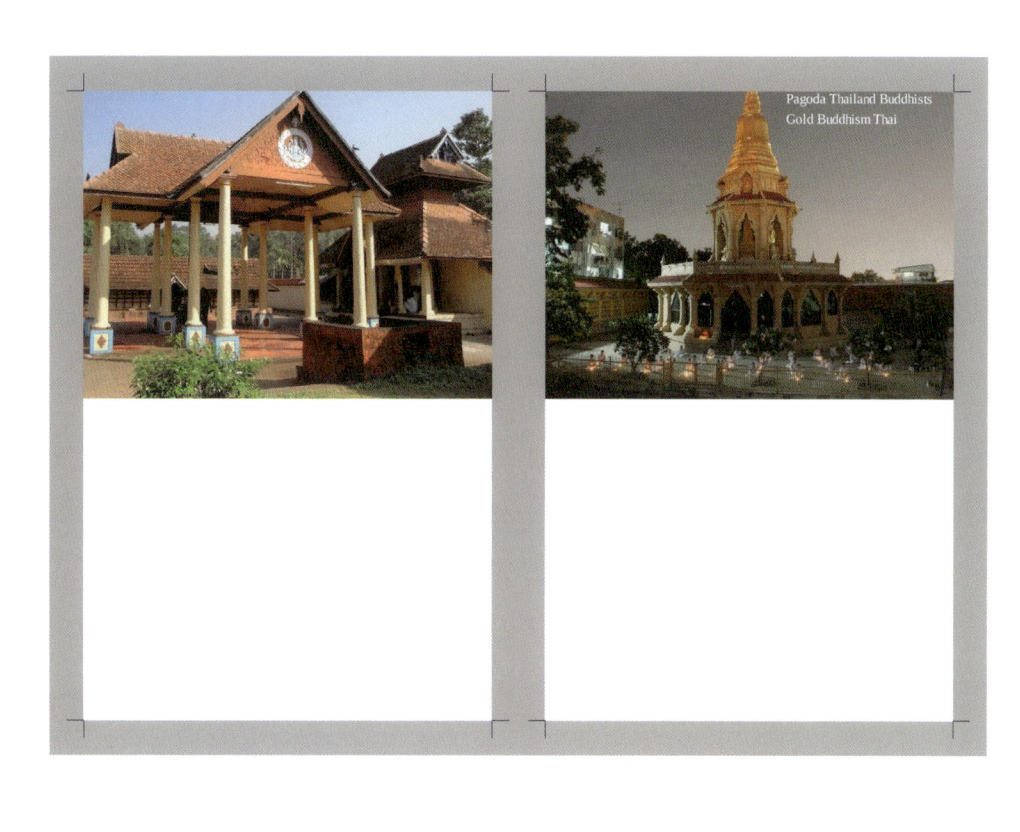

Thailand

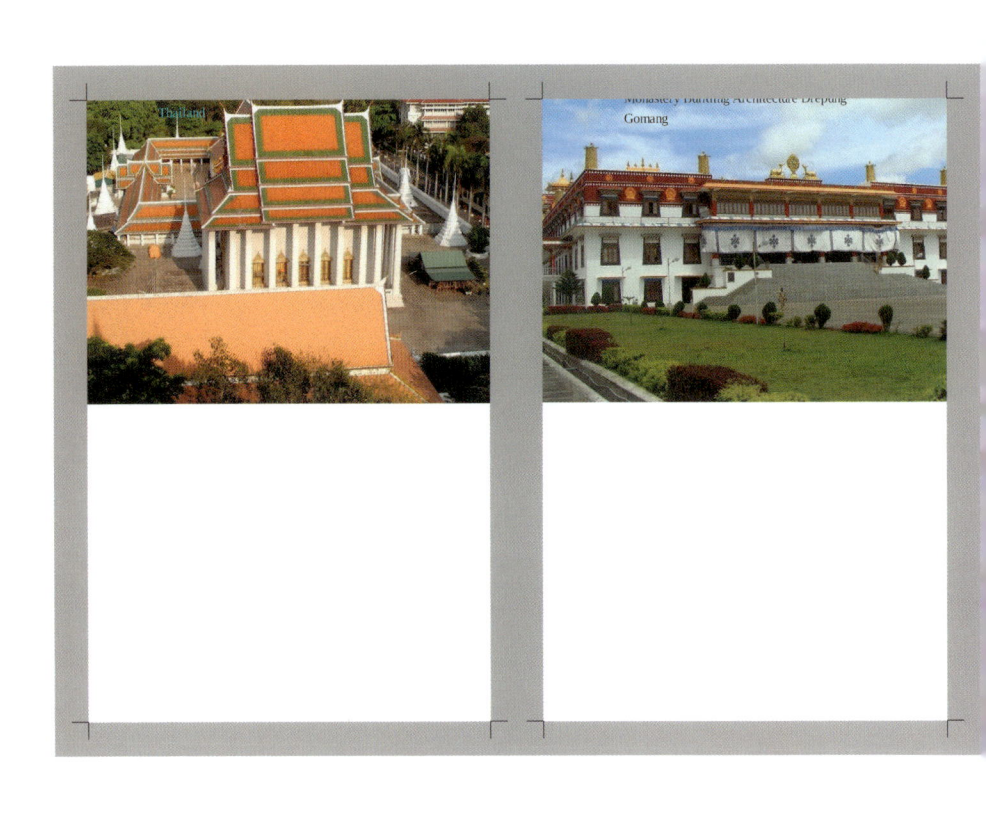

Monastery Building Architecture Drepung Gomang

Pagoda Peace
Buddhist
Battersea
London

Buddhist Measure Adoration
Religion Buddhism

Buddha Architecture

Buddhist Temple Brisbane South Bank Architecture

Buddhist Asia

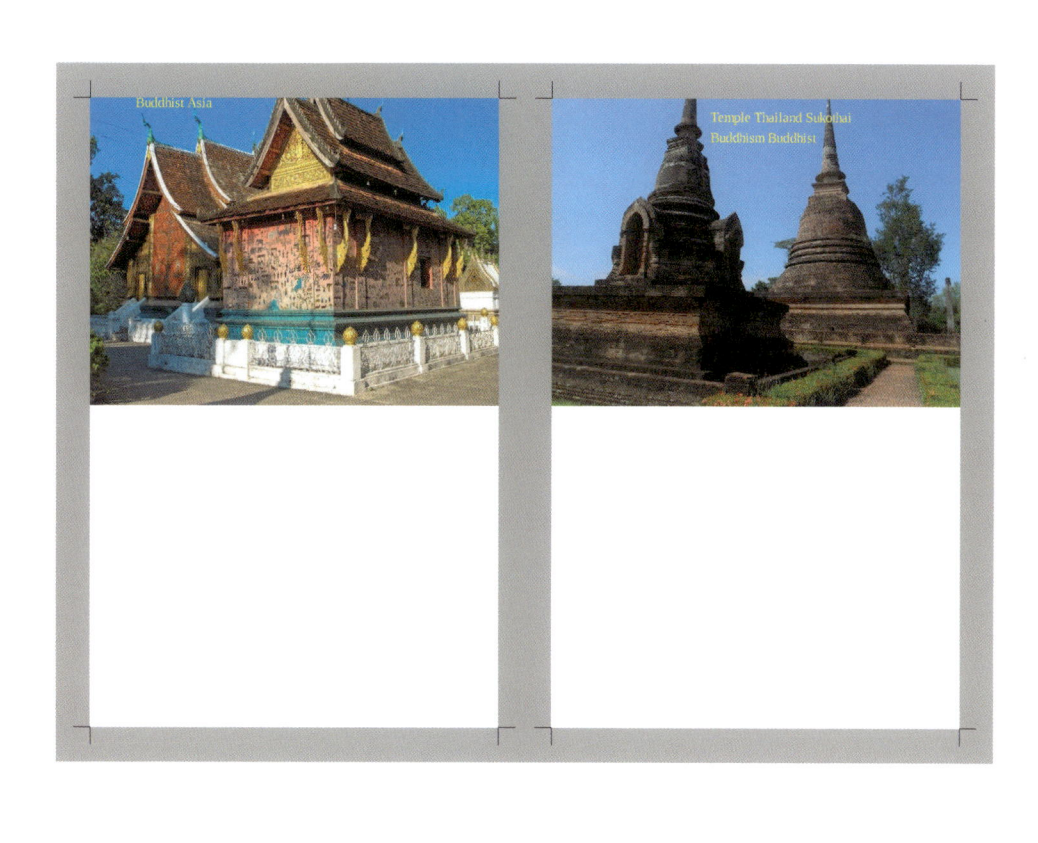

Temple Thailand Sukothai
Buddhism Buddhist

Architecture

Buddhist Temple Religion
Asia Buddhism Travel

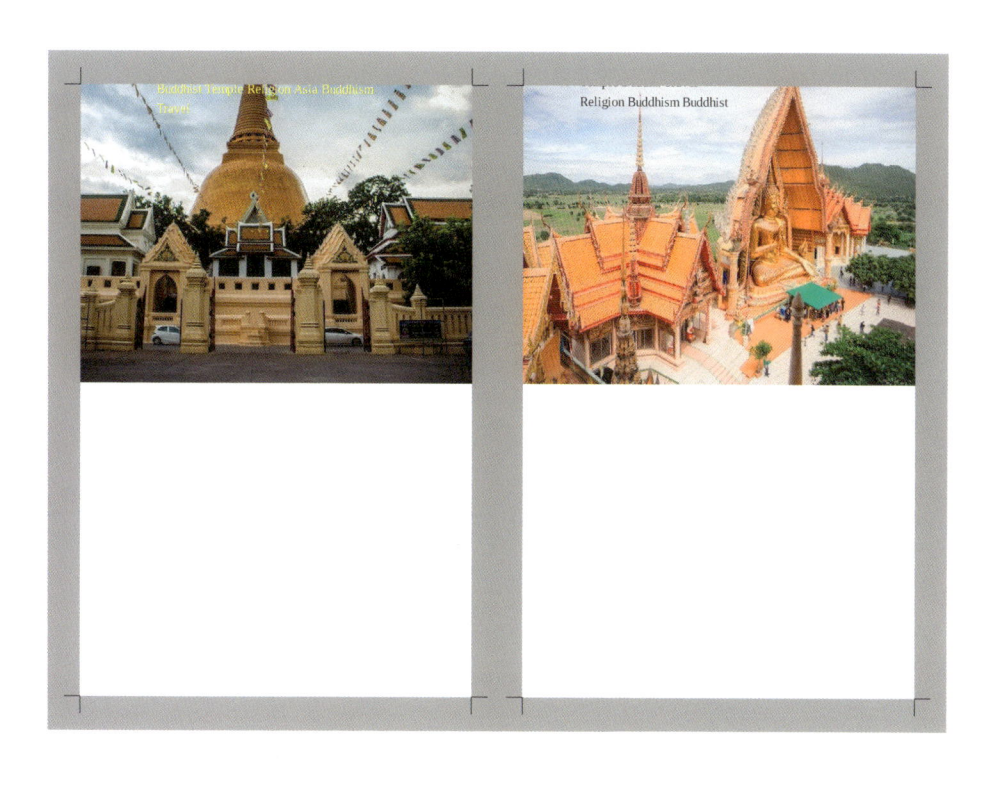

Buddhist Temple Religion Asia Buddhism Travel

Religion Buddhism Buddhist

Old Pagoda Ancient Temple Architecture
Asia

Chiang Rai Thailand

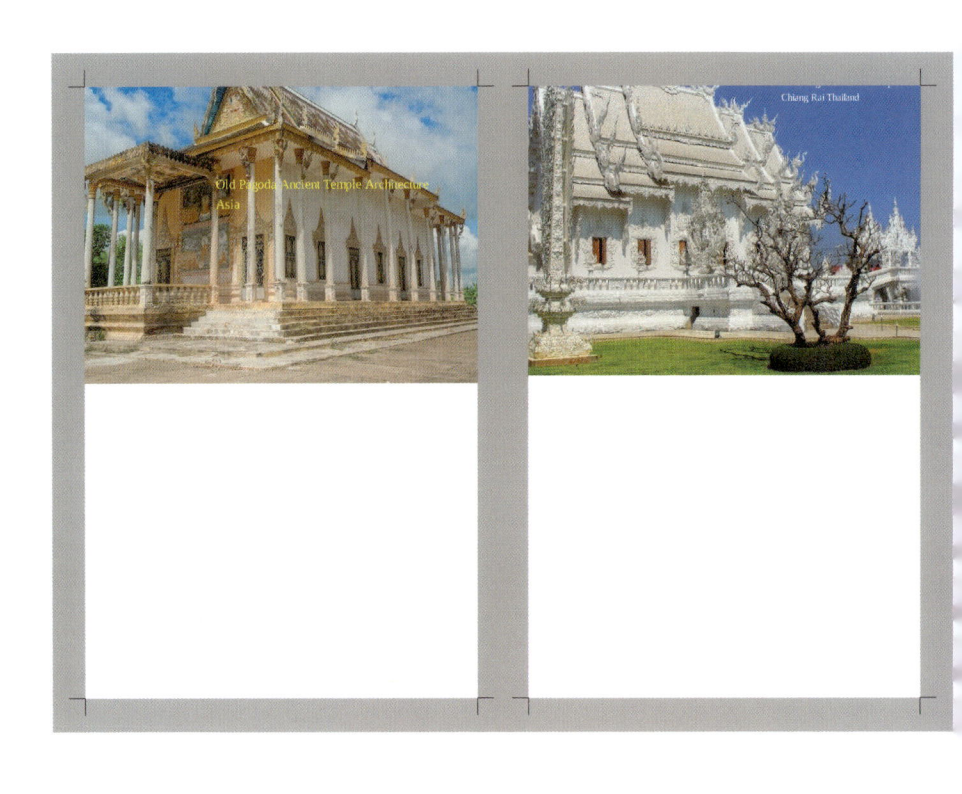

Measure Thailand
Ayutthaya Old
Architecture

Temple Thailand Thai
Temple Buddhist

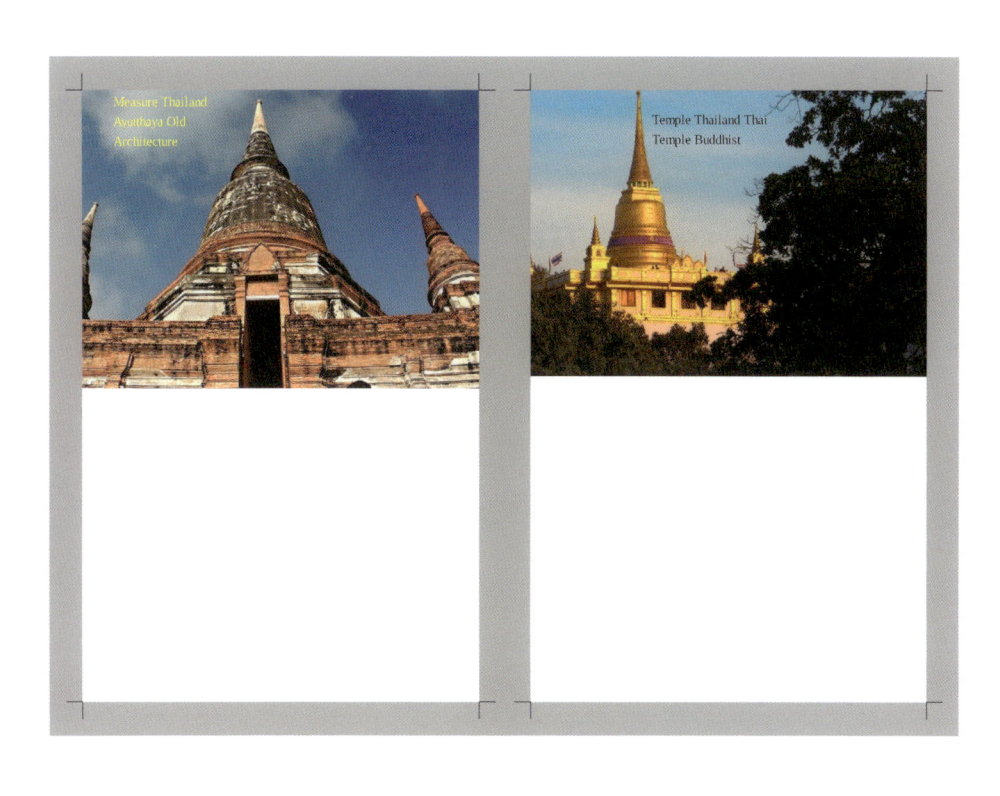

Pattaya Travel Thailand
Buddha Golden Temple

Bangkok

Buddhist

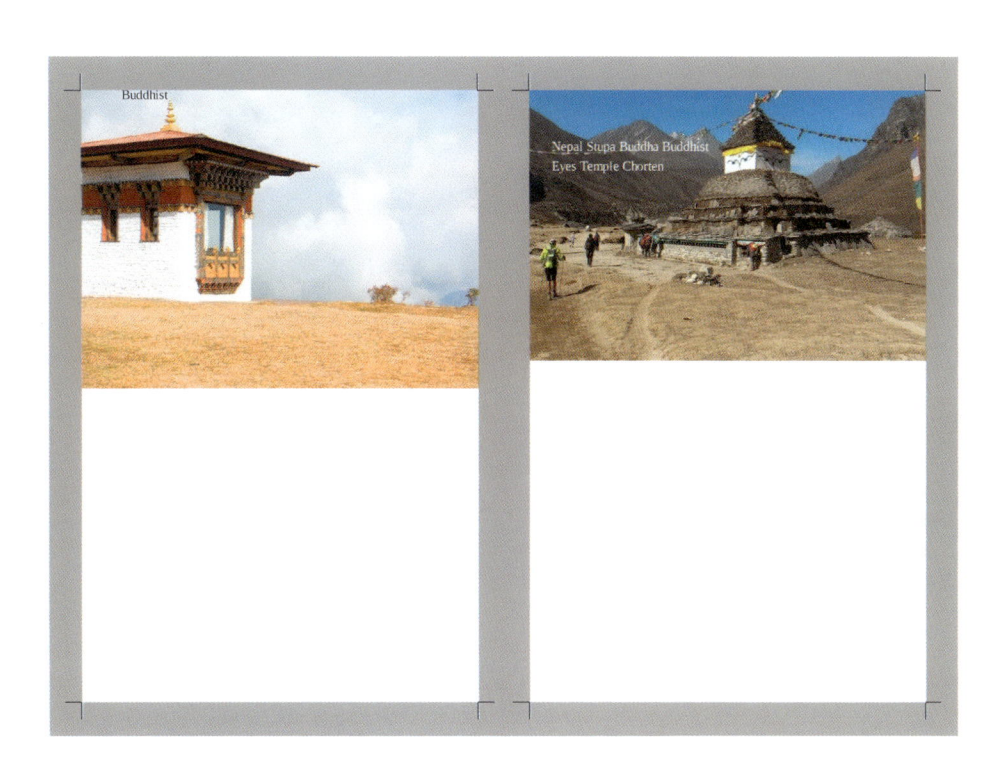

Nepal Stupa Buddha Buddhist Eyes Temple Chorten

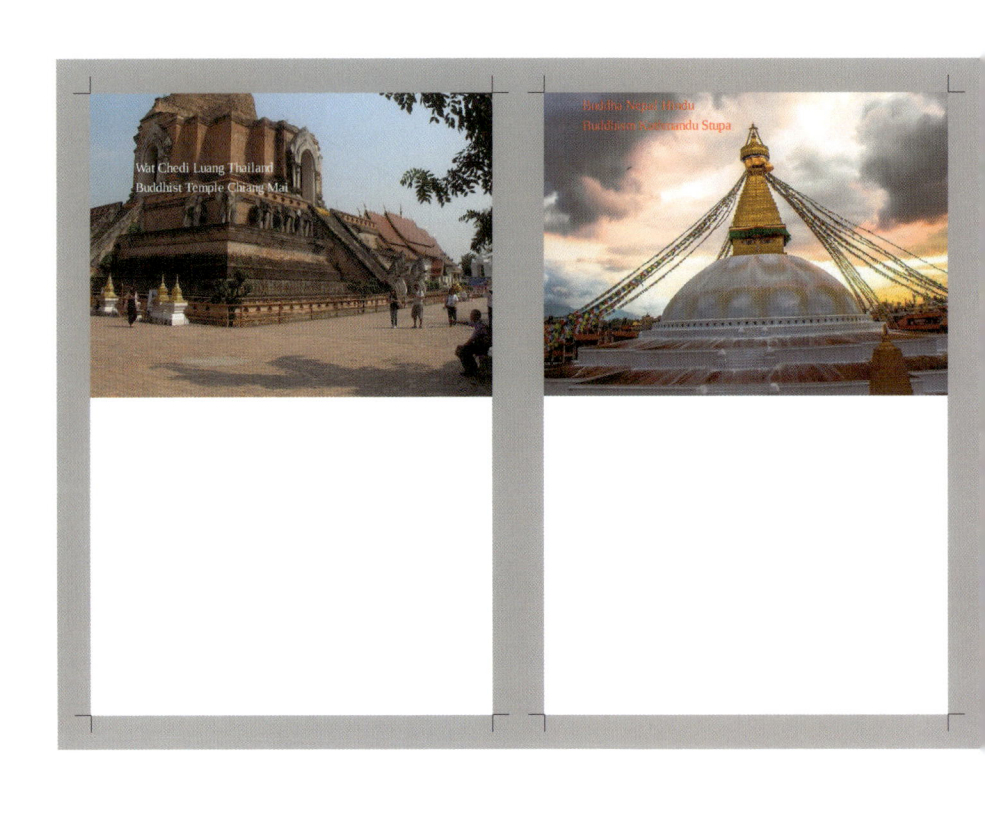

Wat Chedi Luang Thailand
Buddhist Temple Chiang Mai

Bodha Nepal Hindu
Buddhist Boudhanadu Stupa

Taiwan China Temple Buddhism Buddha Religion Asia

Golden Pavilion Japan Kyoto Temple Kinkakuji

God

Taiwan China Temple Buddhism
Buddha Religion Asia

Tokyo Shrine Asakusa Temple Bu Buddhist Japan

ture God Buddhism
hist Asian
odia

Hinduism Religion Prayer
Buddhism God Temple

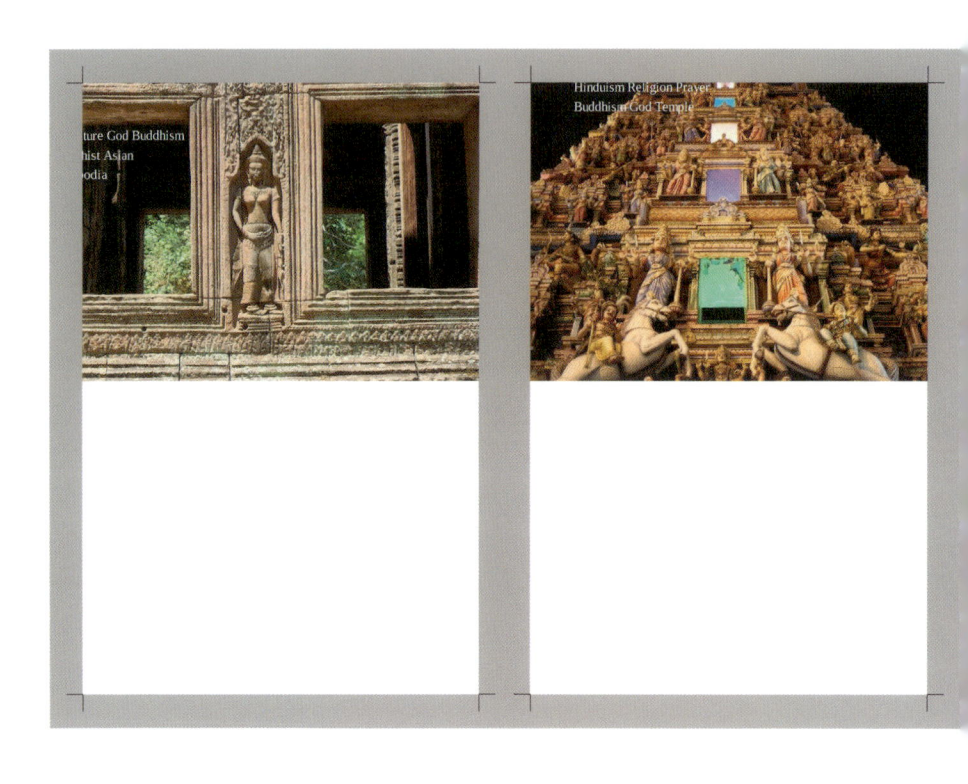

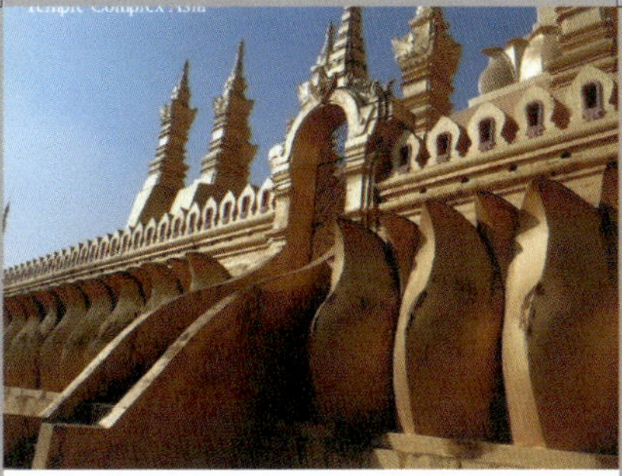

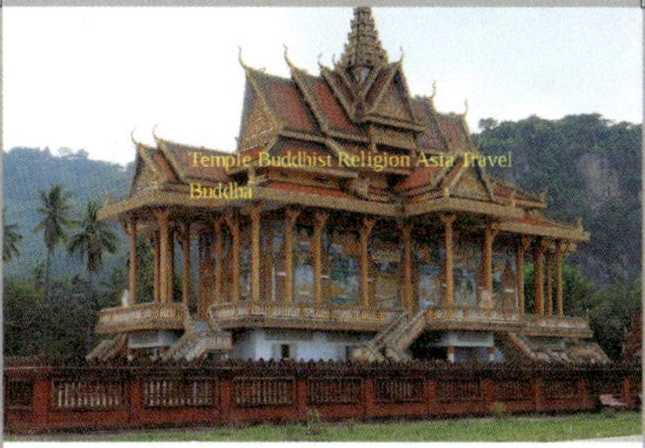
Temple Buddhist Religion Asia Travel
Buddha

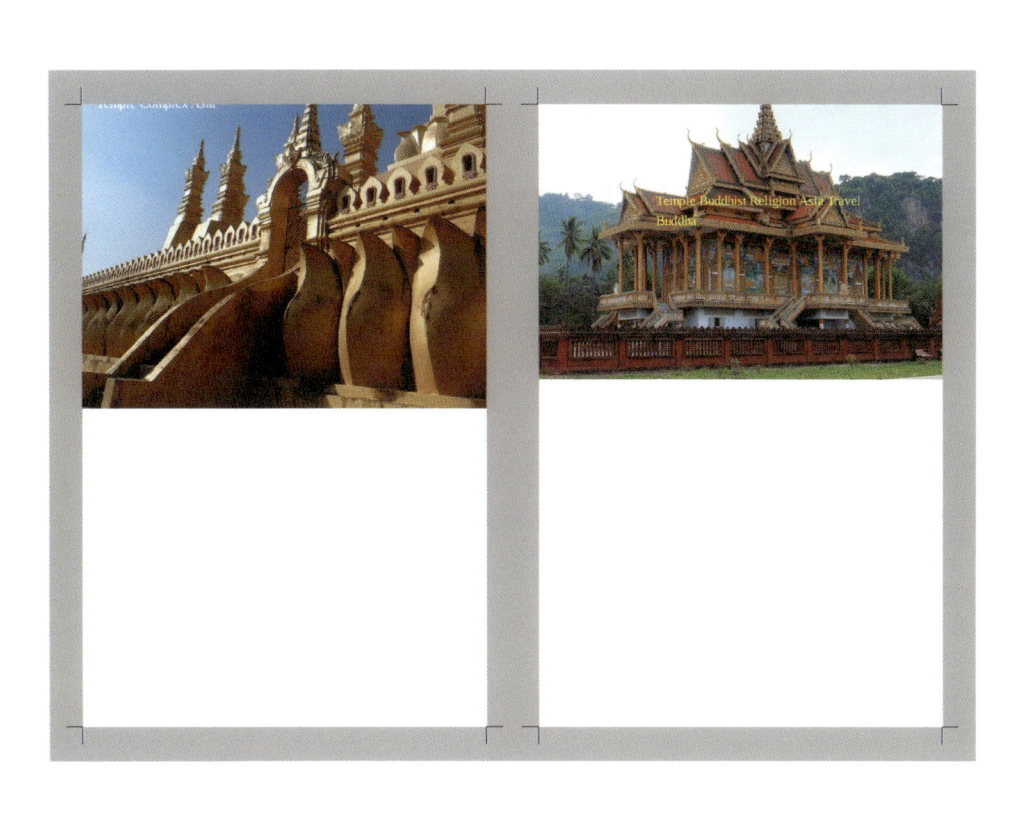

Lot Religion Island

Indonesia Bali Temple Courtyard Buddhist Sacred

Cave Of The Great Buddha 493 Years After Jc

Buddha Thailand Statue Ancient Asia
Buddhism

Temple Thailand Asia Travel Architecture Religion

Indonesia Bali Temple Buddhist Sacred Prayer

Ancient Architecture Art Asia Asian Attraction

Wood

Taiwan Tainan Asia Temple Historically Buddhism

Angkor Wat Temple Twelfth Century Cambodia Asia

Thailand Buddha Temple Asia Religion Buddhism Wat

White Temple Thailand Chiang Rai White Tourism Wat

Indonesia Bali Temple Buddhist
Sacred Prayer

Ginkaku-Ji Temple Garden
Kyoto Japan Buddhist

Complex Buddhist Religion

Temple Nepal Kathmandu Patan Tourism Architecture

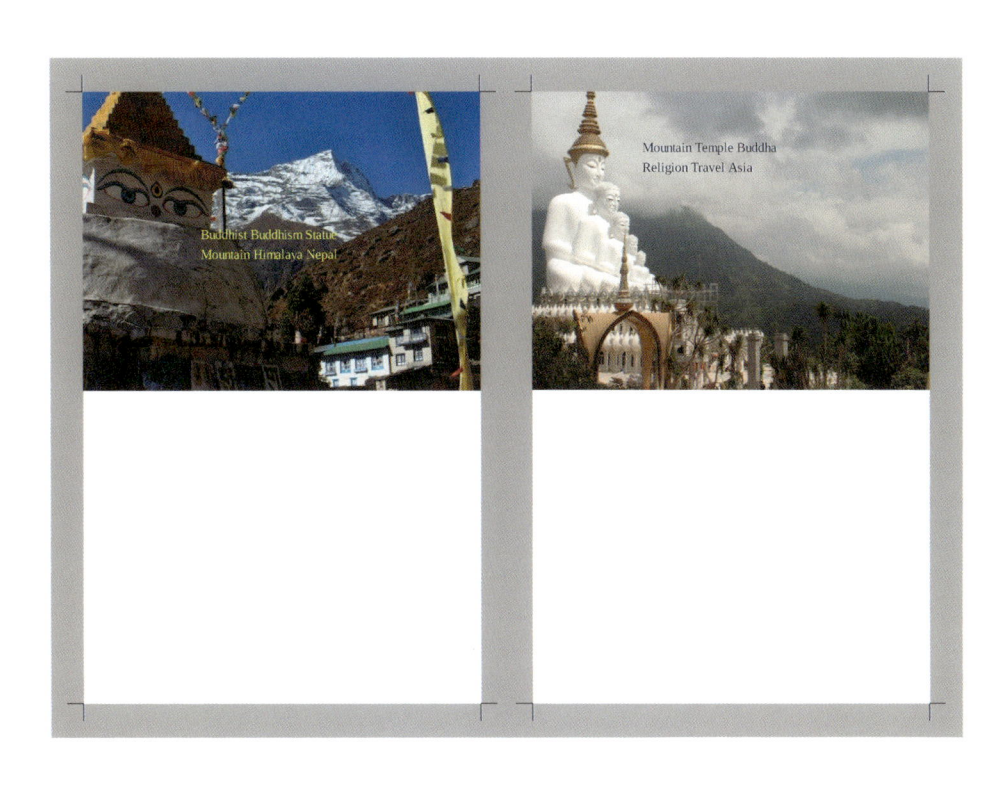

Buddhist Buddhism Statue Mountain Himalaya Nepal

Mountain Temple Buddha Religion Travel Asia

Buddha Photo Blender Statue Buddhist Faith

Temple Buddhist Religion Architecture Landmark

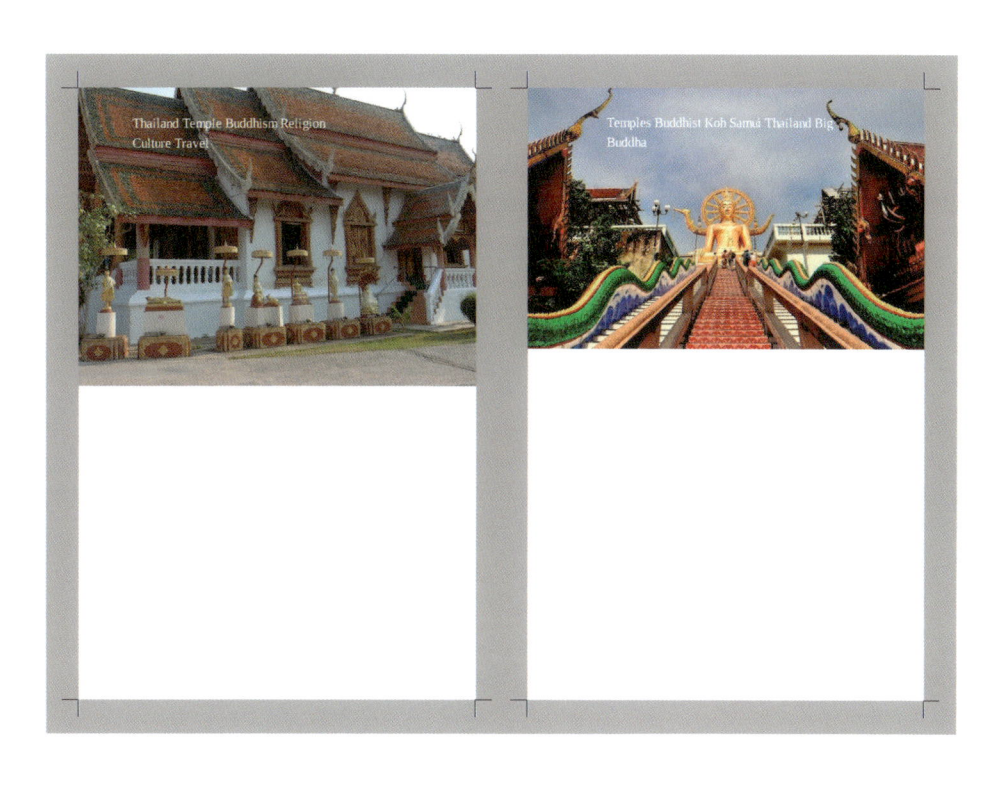

Thailand Temple Buddhism Religion Culture Travel

Temples Buddhist Koh Samui Thailand Big Buddha

Gold

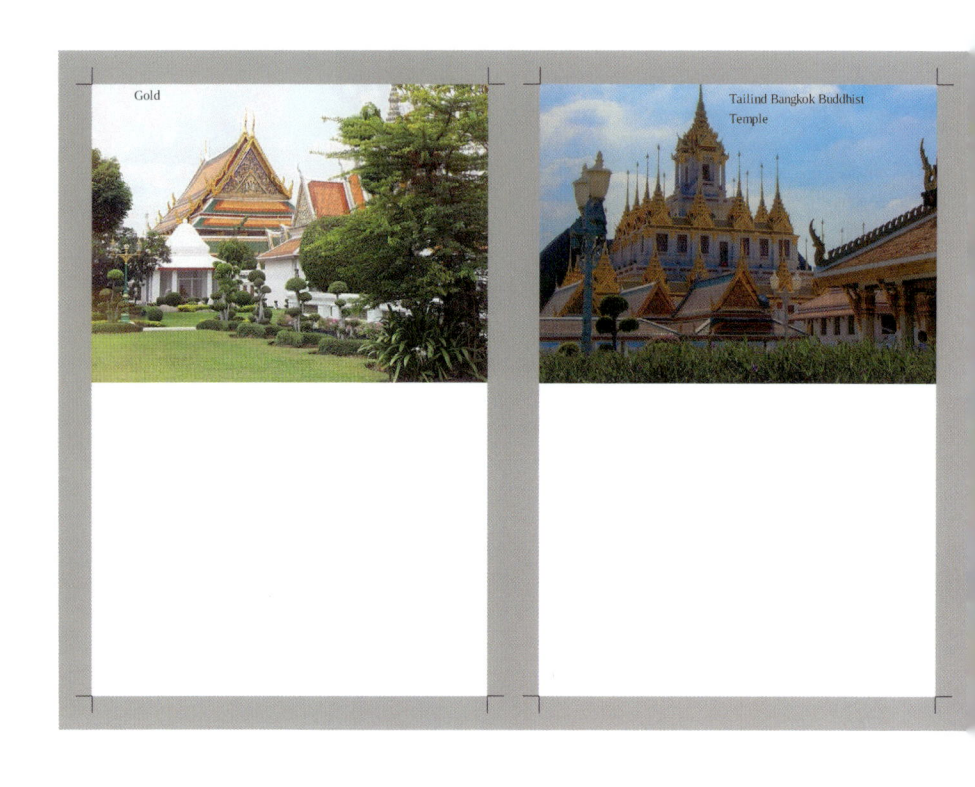

Tailind Bangkok Buddhist Temple

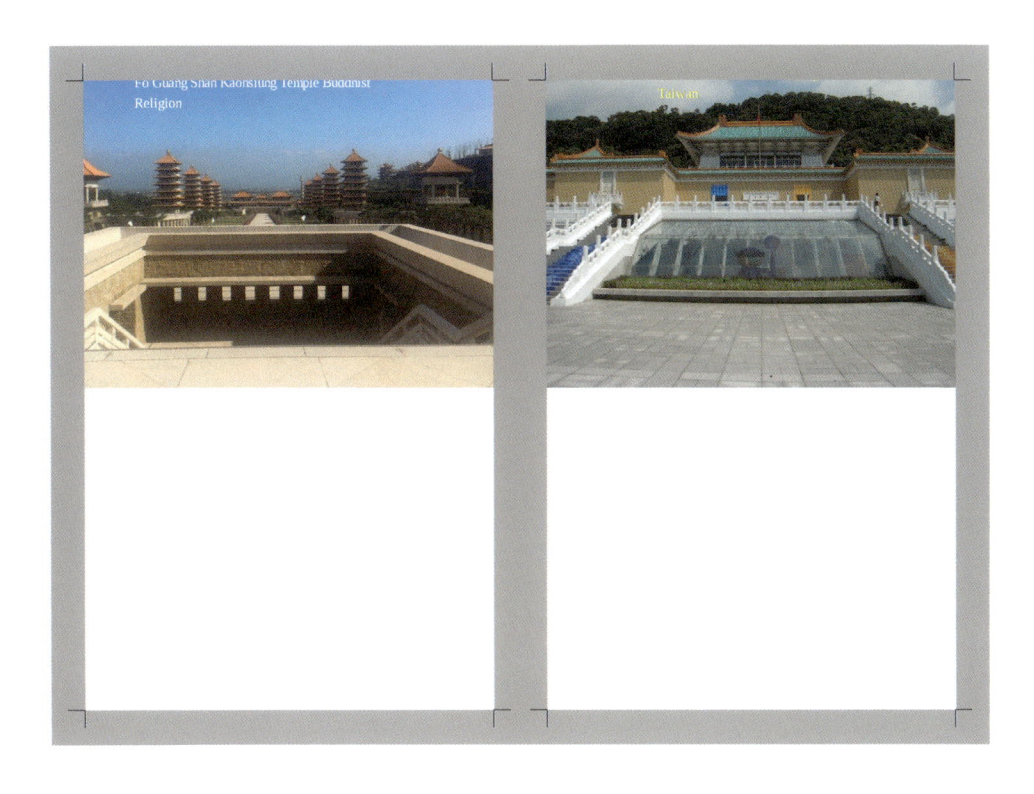

Fo Guang Shan Kaohsiung Temple Buddhist Religion

Taiwan

Inthanon Ancient Architecture Art Asia Background

Agumon's Friends Who Door Portal Asia Temple

Buddhist Temple Buddhism Big Buddha Temple Temple

Bhutan Thimphu As Asia Travel Himalaya Bhutanese

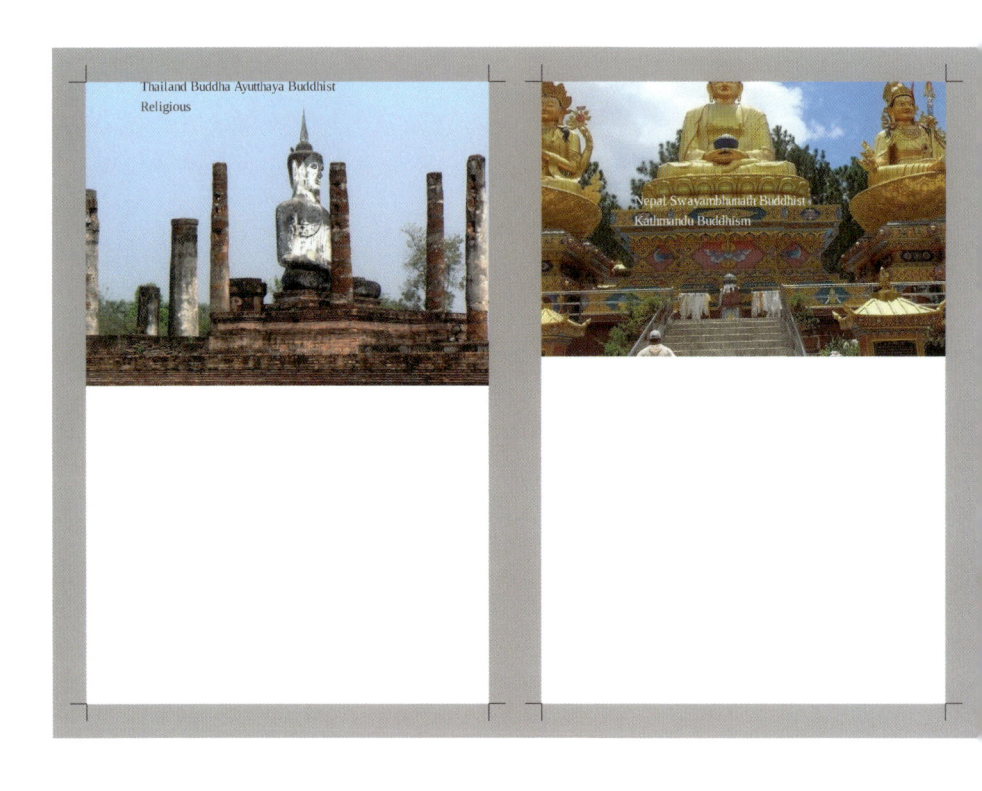

Thailand Buddha Ayutthaya Buddhist Religious

Nepal Swayambhunath Buddhist Kathmandu Buddhism

Sri Lanka Temple Religion
Travel Buddhism Buddhist

Temple Thailand Thai Asia Travel
Bangkok

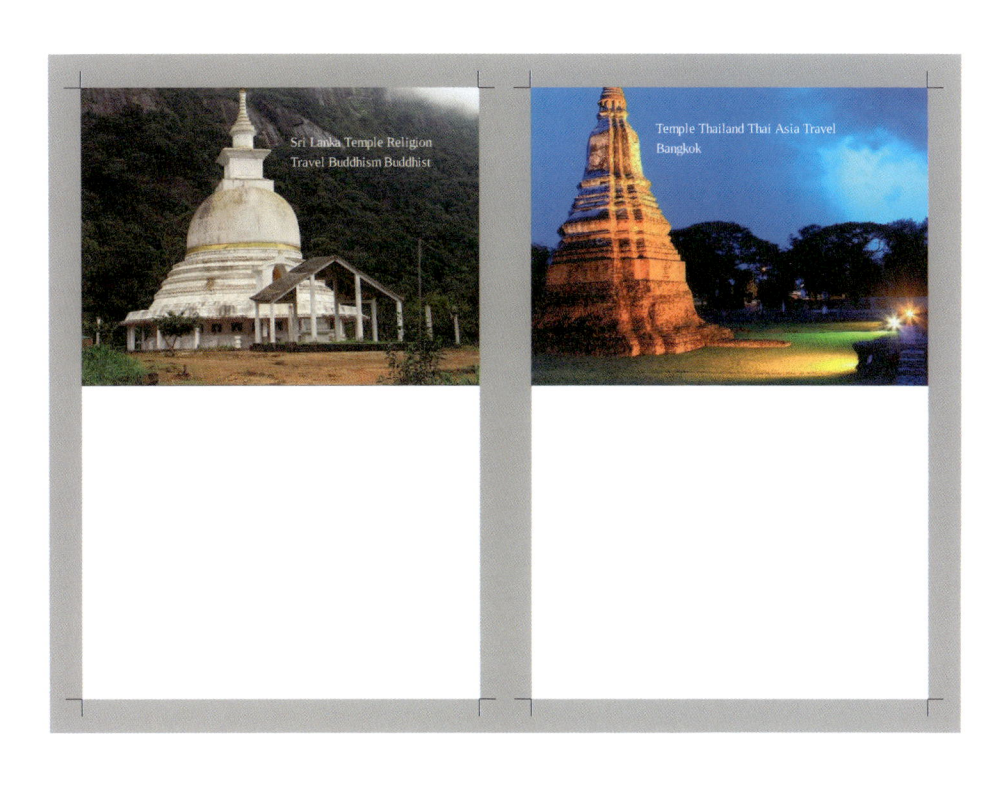

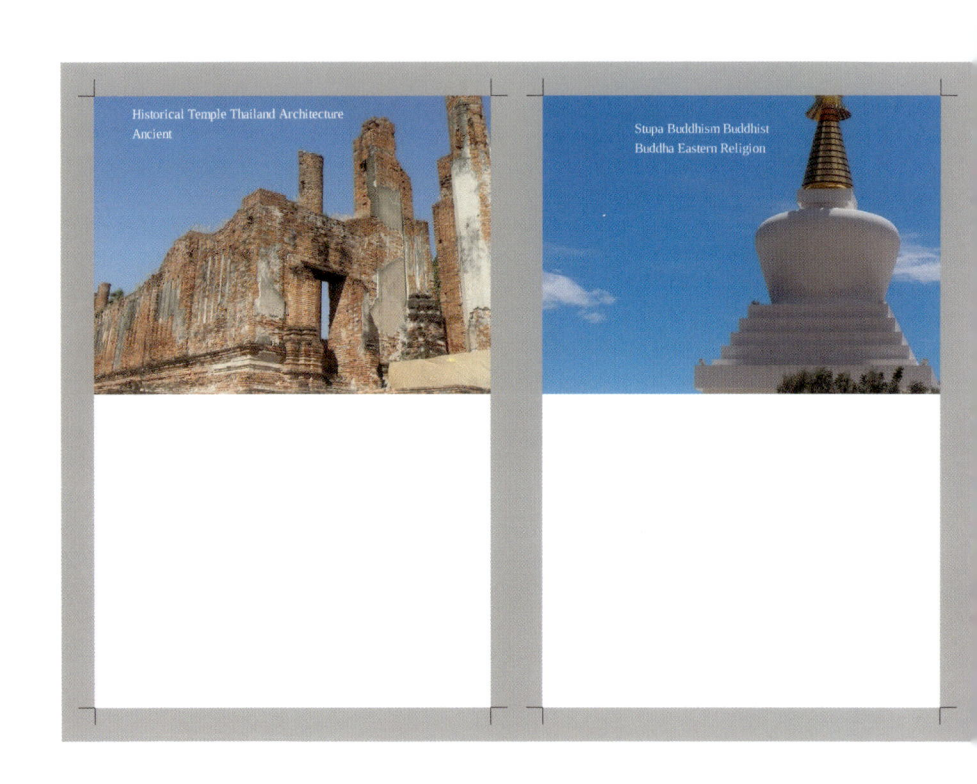

Historical Temple Thailand Architecture Ancient

Stupa Buddhism Buddhist Buddha Eastern Religion

Buddhist Monastery,Monastery Blue Sky

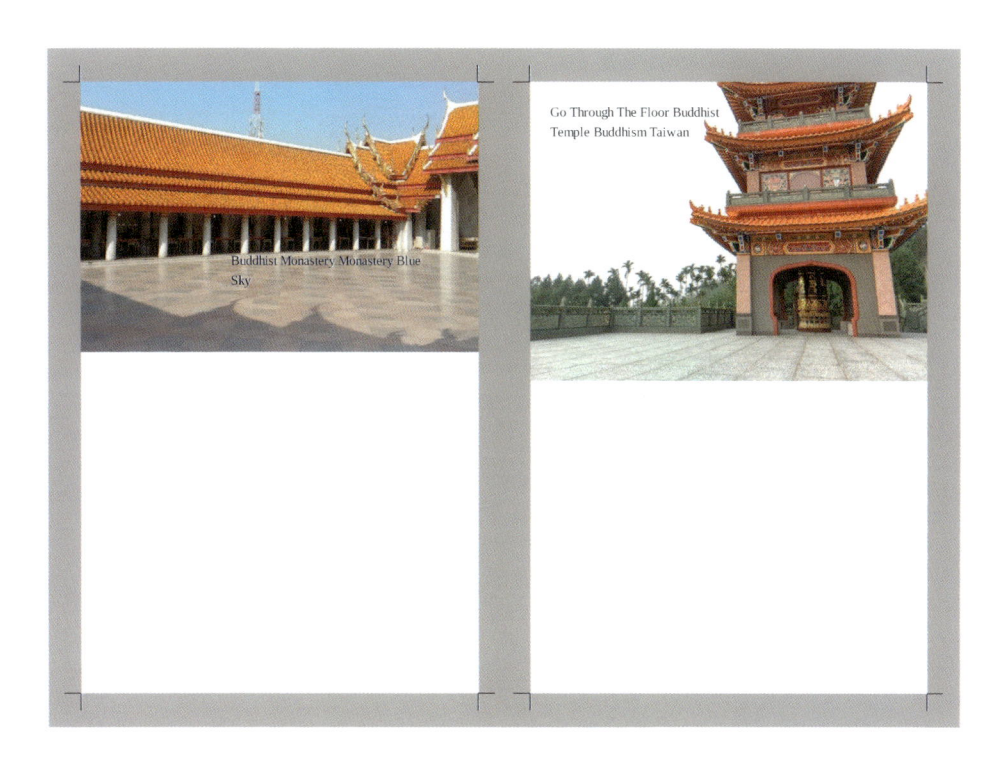

Go Through The Floor Buddhist Temple Buddhism Taiwan

Tibet Lhasa Potala Potala Palace Monastery

Thailand Landmark

Thailand Temple Doré Buddha Religious Sky

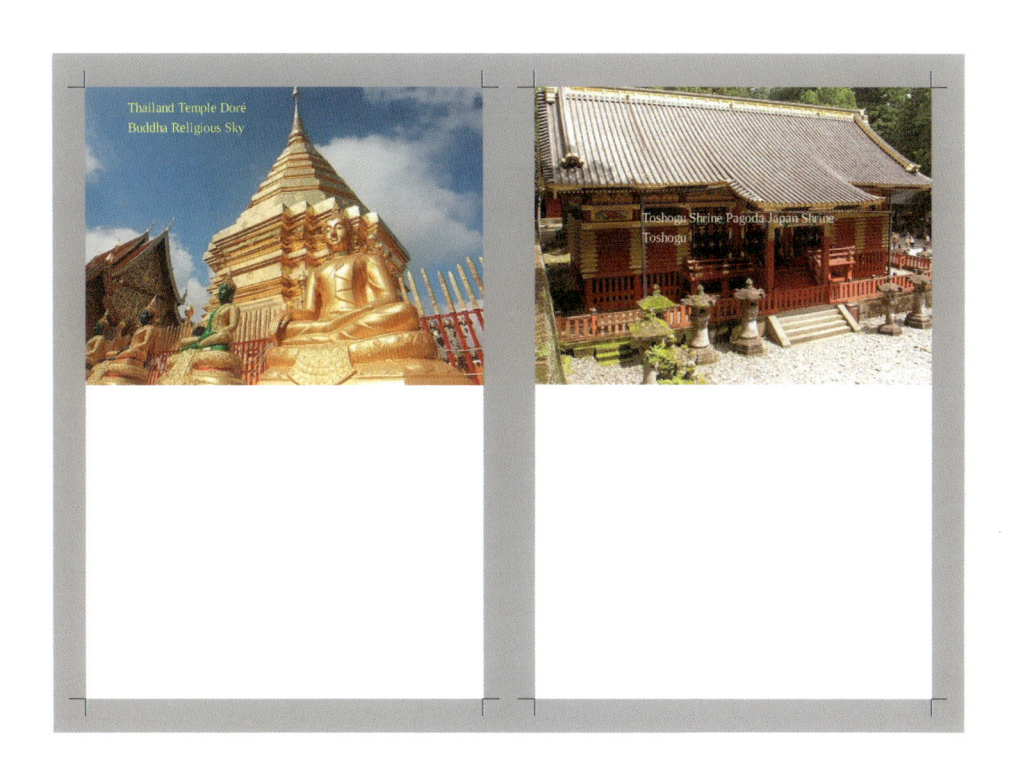

Toshogu Shrine Pagoda Japan Shrine Toshogu

Buddha Religion Asia

Ayutthaya Thailand Ethnicity Sculpture Oriental

Buddha Buddhist

Thailand Buddhist Temple Hua Hin Monastery

Mongolia Temple Buddhist Temple Religion

Architecture

Thailand Temple Church Asia Thai Religion

Asian Religion Ornament Facade Figure Temple

Wen Wu Temple Sun Moon Lake Nantou District Taiwan

Asia Travel

Wat Tham Sua Tiger Cave
Temple Asia Bonita Tour

Burma Myanmar Buddhist

Temple Ornament Asia

Cambodia Ancient Ruins Monument Unesco
Temple

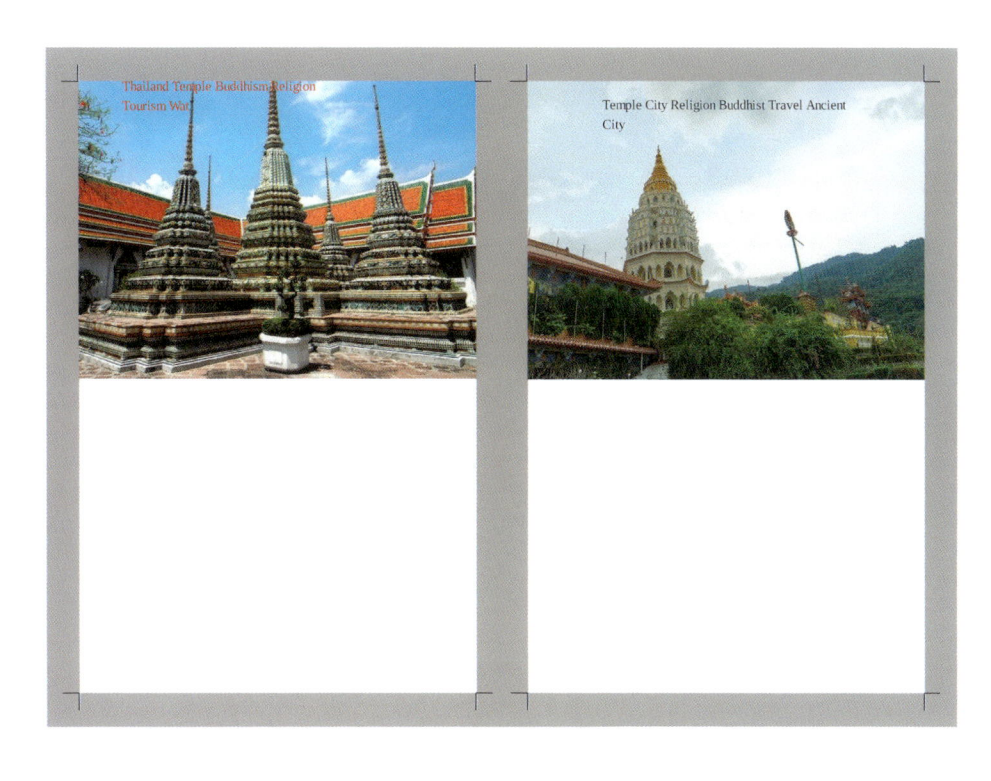

Thailand Temple Buddhism Religion Tourism War

Temple City Religion Buddhist Travel Ancient City

Temple Buddhist Japan Nara East Asia Pagoda

Candi Berahu Mojokerto Jawa Timur Java Indonesian

Temple Thailand Grandpalace Religion Architecture

Borobudur Indonesia Buddhist Sculpture Temple Asia

Ayutthaya Thailand Ethnicity Sculpture Oriental

Monastery Kathmandu Shechen

Stupa Sunset Asia Temple Travel Architecture

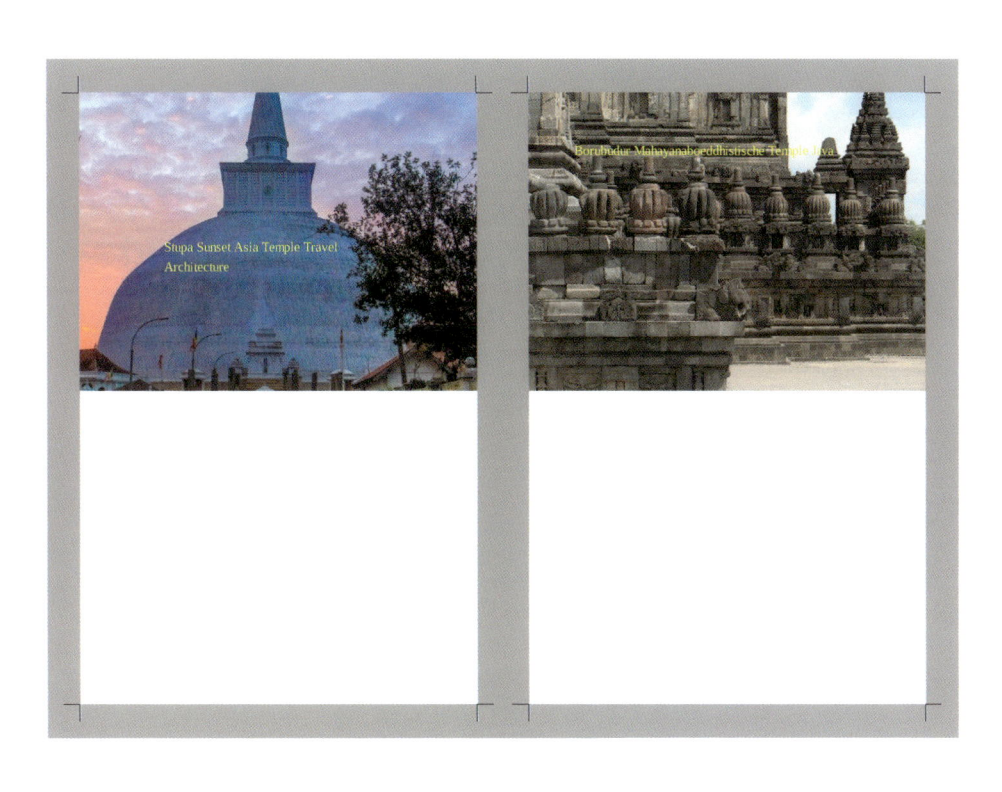

Borobudur Mahayanaboeddhistische Tempel Java

Temple Thailand Wat Travel Buddhism Culture

Angkor Temple Cambodia Wat Siem Reap Hindu

Palace Tibet Tibetan Potala Palace Lhasa China

Adashino Nenbutsuji Kyoto Japan Buddhist Temple

Buddhist Petchaboon Thailand Khaokhor

Temple Buddhism Temple Complex Buddhist Religion

Thailand Temple Art

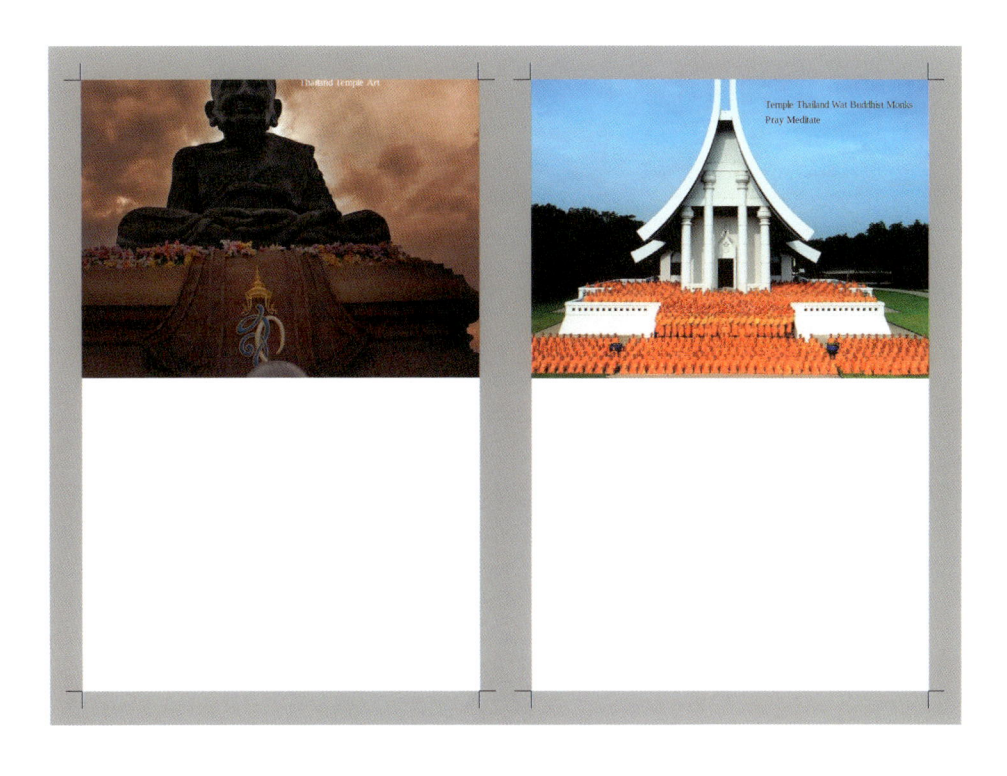

Temple Thailand Wat Buddhist Monks Pray Meditate

Lingshan China Buddhist Buddhism
Religion Faith

Fort Castle Wall Architecture Old Ancient
Tower

Thailand
Ubonratchathani
Monastery Buddhist

Temple Buddha Buddhism
Religion Spiritual

Temple Buddhist Old Rest Meditation

Big Buddha Thailand Phuket Buddhism Statue Big

Vipassana Pagoda Nagpur
Architecture Buddhist

Stupas At Wat Po Temple
Buddhist

Vu Corp Cultural Heritage Ethnic Culture Stone Tower

Bangkok Thailand Wat Pho Palace Buddha Buddhist

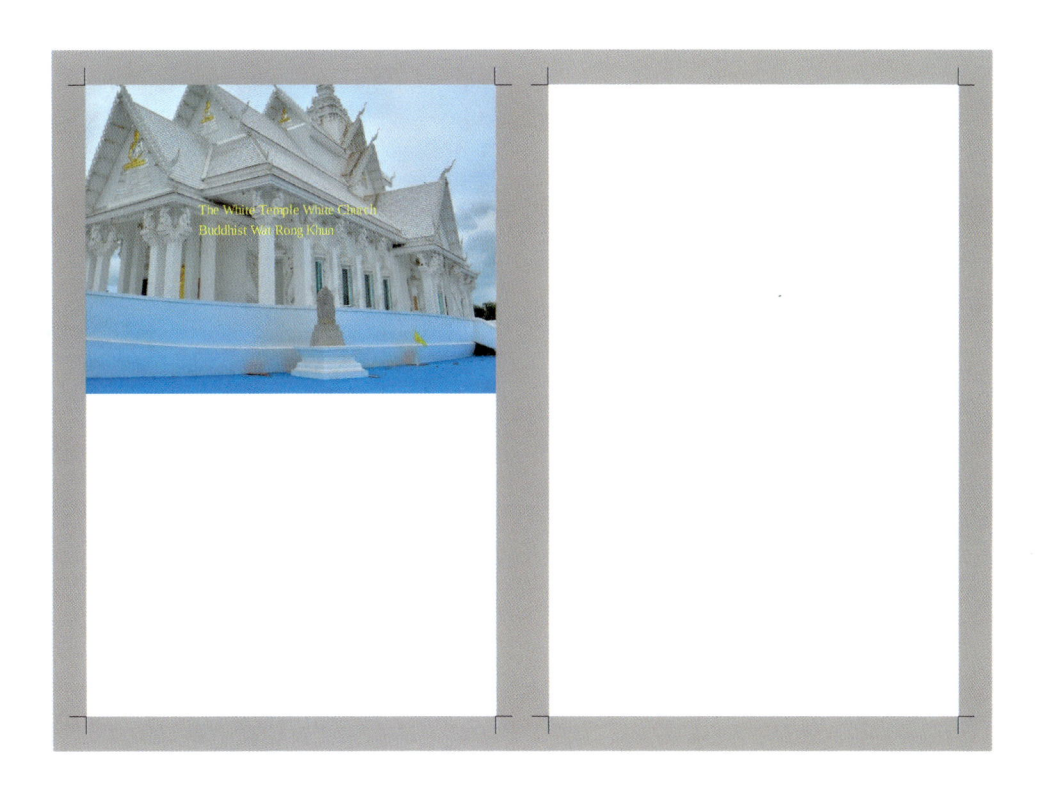

The White Temple White Church
Buddhist Wat Rong Khun

Proof

Printed in Great Britain
by Amazon